FIRST STEPS IN SMALL BOAT SAILING

The Optimist Book

P G HANSEN AND BENT AARRE

FIRST STEPS IN SMALL BOAT SAILING

THE OPTIMIST BOOK

Translation from Danish by Lillan Fuller

ADLARD COLES LIMITED
GRANADA PUBLISHING

London Toronto Sydney New York

First published in Denmark by J. fr. Clausens Forlag
under the title *Optimistjollen.*

This edition published in Great Britain by Granada Publishing
in Adlard Coles Limited, 1970.
Reprinted 1971
Second Edition 1975
Reprinted 1979

Granada Publishing Limited
Frogmore, St Albans, Herts AL2 2NF
and
3 Upper James Street, London W1R 4BP
1221 Avenue of the Americas, New York, NY 10020 USA
117 York Street, Sydney, NSW 2000, Australia
100 Skyway Avenue, Toronto, Ontario, Canada M9W 3A6
110 Northpark Centre, 2193 Johannesburg, South Africa
CML Centre, Queen & Wyndham, Auckland 1, New Zealand

ISBN 0 229 11550 0

Printed in Great Britain by
Fletcher & Son Ltd, Norwich.

Foreword by Robin Knox-Johnston

When I was first asked to write an introduction to this book I knew little either of the Optimist dinghy or the organisation which uses it all over the world to train young people in sailing.

Now, clearly, the International Optimist continues to spread and bring sailing within the reach of many thousands of youngsters. This is a tough, well designed little dinghy, ideally suited to its purpose and I have seen for myself how much fun and good training it provides.

So I am very glad to commend this book which will be useful both to the beginners and to the young sailors as they advance and want to learn the sailing rules.

When you have learnt to sail you may well have the opportunity to compete against and get to know young people from many of the countries I have sailed past.

I hope you enjoy your sailing as much as I do.

Robin Knox-Johnston

About this book

This little book was first published in Danish in 1968 with the title *Optimistjollen*. This was appropriate enough, for Denmark is the European home of the Optimist dinghy, but it would have been a great pity if it had remained in Danish only.

It was clear to those who saw the book, even though they spoke no Danish, that it would appeal to all Optimist helmsmen and women and would indeed also be useful to young people who sail other classes of dinghy. The authors must be congratulated on putting so much information, well illustrated with clear diagrams, into so small a book.

Swedish and Norwegian editions have already been produced, and we are glad now to have an English edition for you.

Since the first English edition of this book was prepared, the Class has spread to many more countries. It is now recommended by the IYRU for juniors up to 15 years of age and in January 1973 this little dinghy became the International Optimist with a new insignia.

To all who read *First Steps in Small Boat Sailing*, whether beginner, average club-sailor sailing mainly for fun or, like the youngsters shown on the jacket, helmsman in international regattas, we wish: Good sailing and good sport.
(The youngsters shown on the jacket are members of the British team at Carantec in northern France; they are seen preparing their boats on the beach at Carantec before one of the races in the Optimist World Championships in 1973.)

J. E. Taylor
Optimist Class Racing Association

Contents

The International Optimist dinghy

Length overall	2·30 m
Waterline length	2·15 m
Beam	1·13 m
Sail area	3·5 sq m
Minimum hull weight	35 kg
Approx total weight	42 kg

The hull is of marine ply on a light frame or alternatively may be of GRP. The Class Rules are controlled by the International Yacht Racing Union (IYRU).

Organisation In Denmark, the European home of this dinghy, the growing Class was controlled by a committee working closely with the national sailing authority — the Danish Sailing Union. A similar pattern of organisation is found in each country sailing the International Optimist: in Great Britain the Class is administered jointly by the Optimist Class Racing Association (OCRA) and the Royal Yachting Association (RYA). Similarly, the International Optimist Dinghy Association (IODA) co-operates with the IYRU to control the Class world-wide.

Regattas The largest event is the ten-day international regatta where young people from many countries sail together and get to know one another. There are very many smaller events, both national and international.

Other information Every Optimist dinghy must be measured and registered before it can take part in class races.

Optimist helmsmen must obey the rules, and particularly the safety rules laid down by the national class authority.

Young helmsmen can take part in class races in their Optimist dinghies until they are 16 years old.

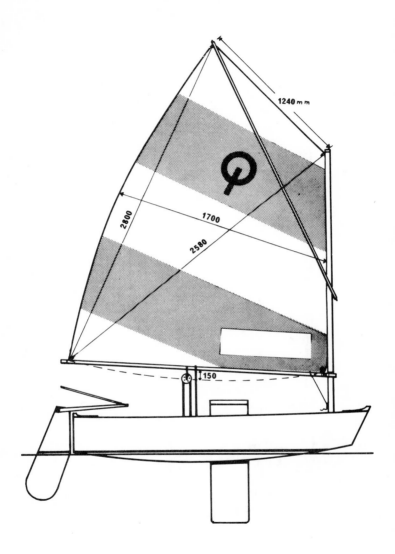

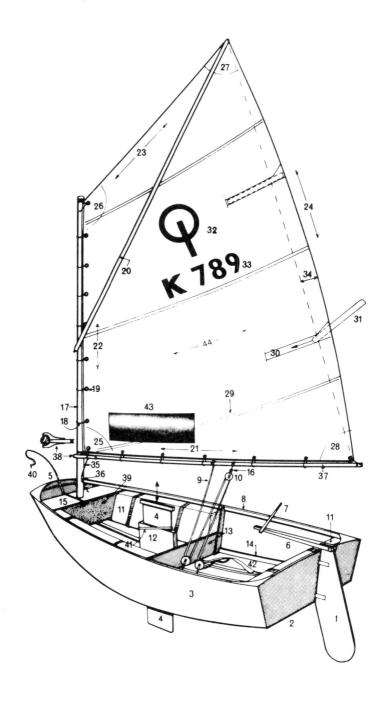

Safety rules

As the Optimist is a small dinghy sailed by children, the Danish Sailing Union decided on the following safety rules

1 The helmsman must be able to swim 220 yards (200 m).
2 There must never be more than one person in the dinghy at a time.
3 The helmsman must always wear a lifejacket.
4 Polystyrene buoyancy was increased in 1971 to three 30 litre blocks: one aft, one each side forward.
5 A plastic bailer must be secured to the dinghy.
6 Optimist dinghies must stay within the sailing areas specified by the clubs.

◀ What do you call that?

1 Rudder
2 Stern transom
3 Side
4 Daggerboard
5 Bow
6 Tiller
7 Tiller extension
8 Gunwale
9 Sheet
10 Pulley block
11 Buoyancy (polystyrene)
12 Daggerboard case
13 Midship frame
14 Chine stringer
15 Mast thwart

16 Swivel
17 Mast
18 Lacing
19 Cringle
20 Sprit
21 Foot
22 Luff
23 Head
24 Leech
25 Tack
26 Throat
27 Peak
28 Clew
29 Seam
30 Batten pocket
31 Batten
32 Class insignia

33 Sail number and national letter
34 Roach
35 Downhaul
36 Cleat
37 Boom
38 Boom jaw
39 Mast thwart bulkhead
40 Painter
41 Shock-cord for holding daggerboard in place
42 Toe strap
43 Window in sail
44 Sail panel

The Danish safety rules, set out on the previous page, are varied slightly from country to country. In England, bag buoyancy is allowed as an alternative to the polystyrene type, and there is no fixed rule about how far a child must be able to swim before being allowed to start to sail. Other important rules are left to the discretion of the clubs as local conditions vary so much. Club rules normally require an officer of the day to be in charge of all the children under instruction, and to make provision for safety boats.

Even though the Optimist dinghy is very stable and is not likely to capsize, the young helmsman must be told, before going afloat for the first time, what to do if he or she does capsize.

In Great Britain, clubs award the Optimist Badge to their young helmsmen who complete a beginners' course. Stars—first, second and third—are added to the badge as the helmsmen improve their standard, and these awards are closely linked to the RYA Proficiency Scheme. Senior Optimist helmsmen can qualify as RYA Instructors. Other countries have similar systems to encourage training; seamanship and safety always complement racing.

How it all began

The Optimist dinghy was designed by Clark Mills in 1947 for the members of a youth club at Clearwater in Florida. Why did he do this? The members of the club had been fitting sails to their soap-boxes to race them in the streets— a very dangerous sport! Clark Mills's idea was to give them an exciting but safer sport on the water.

The Optimist spread quickly in America and in 1954 a Danish architect, Axel Damgaard, read an article about it in an American magazine. This seemed to him to be the ideal dinghy for the young people of Denmark, so he and a few friends, members of the Vordingborg Sailing Club built four or five Optimists between them that year. Complete with sail they cost just £15 each. The new Danish Optimists lived up to their builders' expectations, and soon these dinghies were being made all over the country; building classes were started and the newspapers helped spread news and information about the dinghy.

The next big year in the story of the growth of the Class was 1957. Summer schools were started with help from Olympic Gold Medal winner Paul Elvström, and a series of regattas was started for Optimist helmsmen from all over Denmark. The first meeting between Denmark and Norway was in 1959 and the following year Swedish Optimists joined in the international races.

It was in 1960 that an organisation was set up to control Optimist sailing in Denmark; there were over 2,000 Optimists divided among forty-four clubs. Nine area representatives formed the central committee.

International racing. Visitors to Denmark were often impressed by the Optimist sailing they saw there, and so it was that the class came to be started in countries outside Scandinavia. Optimists appeared in England in 1961 and, in 1962, Nigel Ringrose invited teams from Denmark, Norway, Sweden and Germany to a week's racing and sight-seeing based on the Hamble river. This experiment proved to be very popular both with the young helmsmen and with the team leaders and was the first of a series of regattas which has continued each year since then. In 1963 Sweden was the host nation for a regatta at Göteborg, while the 1964 regatta at Aarhus in Denmark was notable for the participation of an American team.

The 1965 regatta was especially important because the team leaders at this regatta held at Abo in Finland decided that the time had come to form an international organisation; IODA was set up with Viggo Jacobsen of Denmark as Chairman.

The International Optimist Dinghy Organisation. What were the aims of this new international organisation? As Viggo Jacobsen explains:

'IODA was formed in 1965 at the international regatta in

13

Abo to ensure that the Optimist dinghies being built in more and more countries were all of the same design. The second aim was to maintain contact between the countries which were using the Optimist dinghy for junior sailing, and finally the organisation was charged with making the arrangements for future international regattas. Membership was open to countries which wished to take part in the international regattas and to organise these events on their own waters in turn.'

The 1966 regatta was the first held outside Europe; it took place in Miami, USA and was very much enjoyed by the young helmsmen from Europe.

In 1967, the regatta was held in Austria, on the Neusiedlersee and at Carantec in Brittany in 1968. It had grown enormously from that small affair on the Hamble in 1962 when the international regatta returned to England in 1969, but the same spirit of competition and friendship between young people of many lands still marked the ten-day meeting. Since then, Germany and Switzerland have joined the lengthening list of host nations for this annual event.

International status

This big step for the Class in 1973 has led to closer co-operation between IODA and the IYRU, particularly to meet IODA's first aim, and was the logical outcome of the remarkable international expansion of this class of small but tough dinghies for young people.

Getting your dinghy ready

You can learn a lot about how to rig your Optimist by looking at the diagram on page 10. The following remarks will also help you.

The downhaul (35 on page 10) is used to pull down the boom and so keep the luff of the sail taut. A spliced loop at one end of the downhaul fits round the boom-jaw and the other is secured to a jam cleat (figure 1), or to an ordinary cleat (figure 2).

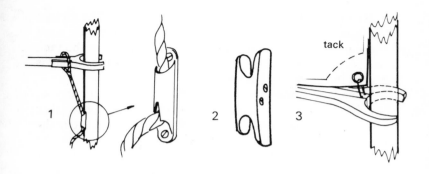

The small holes are drilled in the boom-jaws close to the mast and are used for lashing the tack of the sail to the boom (figure 3). The sprit may be kept up by means of a rope strop with eyes at both ends (figure 4) placed around the mast and engaged on a toothed rack (figure 5). The end of the sprit is placed in the smaller eye. The rack may be made of wood with teeth about 2 cm apart, or a plastic rack can be bought from a chandler. The ends of the sprit will be shaped to stop them working through the eyes (as, for example, in figure 6).

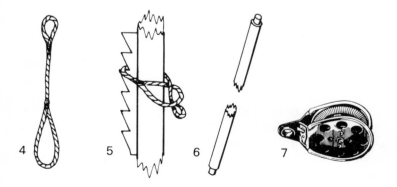

By raising the sprit you can tighten the sail. The picture opposite shows a correctly set sail. With a following wind there will be a crease from the top of the sprit to the tack of the sail. This crease will disappear when the boom is pulled in for sailing up wind.

When you come to secure the sail to the mast and boom, it is best to use a short piece of line for each cringle rather than a long line laced along the spars. Do not fasten the ties too tightly. Don't forget to put the battens into the pockets in the leech of the sail; they keep the sail a good shape and stop the leech flapping when you are sailing.

The rope you use to hold and adjust the sail is called the sheet. In the diagram on page 10 you will see the sheet rigged for fresh winds; it passes through three blocks, two of which are on the hog. In a light wind, when the pressure of the wind on the sail is not so great, you can manage with only one block.

On the other hand, when you are experienced enough to sail in strong winds and to take part in long races, you will find that, even with three blocks, it becomes hard work to keep the sheet pulled in. You will then want to fit a special block, a ratchet block, which helps you hold the sheet but does not jam and so still enables you to release the sheet quickly when you need to do so. The ratchet block will be the one on the hog nearest to your hand. One type is shown in figure 7 (page 15).

Construction

Wooden or GRP Optimists may be purchased ready made from builders, or you may be able to purchase an unfinished hull and complete it yourself.

Many Optimist dinghies are constructed at home, either from kits supplied by the builders or direct from the plans. This is not difficult and indeed it is possible to complete a kit in about twenty-four hours of work, but since the dinghy must conform to the plans and dimensions and its

Down-wind technique in a light wind: lift the sail and reduce the hull drag by heeling windward. Not a trick for beginners.

Photograph by Eileen Ramsay

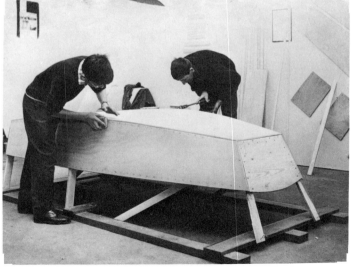

measurements must be within the tolerances shown on the measurement form, the work must be done carefully. The early stages are particularly important.

The bow and stern transoms, together with the midships frame, all with their side-pieces extended to form building 'legs', are used as a building frame. These must, therefore, first be made and set up accurately at the spacing shown on the plans. If you purchase a kit, these three will be supplied to you already assembled. You must have a rigid base to work on and the form of this building base is also shown on the plans. Be careful to check the distances between the frames before you go any further. Make sure also that the temporary battens used to hold the frames in place are strong enough and well secured.

This system of building the dinghy around the three frames is sensible and economical when only one Optimist is being built; an accurate hull should result if care is taken. On the other hand if the members of a club, for example, intend to build a small batch of Optimists, it is better to set up a building jig. In this way it is easier to ensure that all the dinghies will be close to mid-tolerance in their dimensions, and the time taken to construct the jig is repaid in time saved on completing the hulls.

The sail numbers are supplied by the class association and the completed dinghy must carry its number on all its separate parts. Don't forget to carve the number in the hog before varnishing it!

Finally, the completed dinghy must be measured and the measurement form sent to the class association so that the dinghy can be registered as an Optimist.

The pictures opposite show two steps in the building of an Optimist hull at home. You will enjoy sailing your own boat even more if you have helped to build her yourself.

Your sail

The sail will drive your dinghy along best if, instead of

being flat, it has the shape shown in figure 7. You will see that the curvature is greatest next to the mast and gradually decreases aft. Both the luff and the foot of the sail are cut on a curve to help the sail take up the proper shape. The leech is also curved, but that is only to make the sail larger (figure 8).

Nowadays, most sails are made from Terylene (called

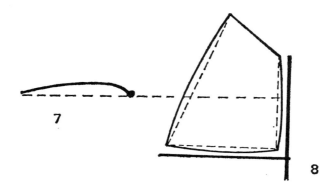

Dacron in America) instead of cotton. Terylene is very strong and your sail will stand up to a lot of wear and tear, but you must still look after it. When you have finished sailing, take off the sprit and roll the sail round the mast. Keep the sail in a dry place and remember that if it is wet it must be allowed to air, so do not roll it too tightly.

The proper Optimist sails are made by professional sail-makers.

Dirty Sails. The best thing is to keep the sail clean. Do not let it touch the ground, and and try to keep it out of oil-covered water. Rinse salt off regularly with fresh water. For general soiling, wash with a stiff brush and warm soapy water. Remove tar or oil with a household stain remover and rinse out afterwards.

Bends and hitches

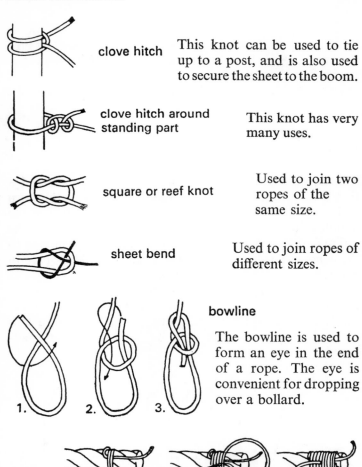

clove hitch This knot can be used to tie up to a post, and is also used to secure the sheet to the boom.

clove hitch around standing part This knot has very many uses.

square or reef knot Used to join two ropes of the same size.

sheet bend Used to join ropes of different sizes.

bowline

The bowline is used to form an eye in the end of a rope. The eye is convenient for dropping over a bollard.

1. 2. 3.

whipping 1. 2. 3.

If you whip the end of a rope it does not fray out.
Nylon and Terylene rope can be sealed with a match.

Learning to sail

The first time you go on the water, there seem to be so many things to do at once and it certainly pays to start on a day when there is not too much wind. With the dinghy moving slowly and quietly, you will have time to see how it reacts to rudder movements and to the way you adjust the sail.

Where to sit in the dinghy

The Optimist sails best when it is properly trimmed— that is when it is not down by the bow, down by the stern or heeled over to one side. So you sit more or less in the middle of the dinghy. When the pressure of the wind on the sail makes the boat heel over, you balance it by moving to the windward side (the side away from the sail). Be careful never to sit on the lee side, unless the wind is very light indeed (in which case you can help to keep the sail a good full shape by using your weight to heel the dinghy to lee-ward). All the time you are sailing, you must take care to see that your position in the boat keeps it properly balanced.

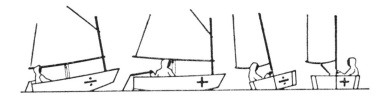

Steering with the rudder

You will get the feel of the dinghy if you hold the tiller lightly between your thumb and index finger. Make small, gentle adjustments with the tiller to keep the dinghy on course. If you move the tiller violently, the rudder acts as a brake and slows the dinghy.

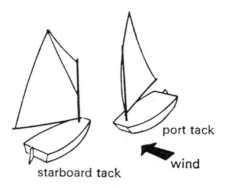

port tack

wind

starboard tack

Port and starboard. The port side is the left side of the dinghy as you face forwards, the starboard side is the right side. When the wind blows on the port side of the dinghy, you say you are on the port tack, when it blows on the starboard side, on the starboard tack. The sail and boom will, of course, be on the other side — to starboard when you are on the port tack.

Changing from one tack to the other — you can do this in one of two ways.

1 *Tacking* This means that you turn the bow towards the wind and continue turning the same way until the sail fills again on the new tack. This is how you do it: push the tiller away from you towards the lee side of the dinghy and the dinghy will turn up into the wind (this is called luffing); pass carefully under the boom, changing hands with tiller and sheets, just as the dinghy is passing through the eye of the wind; when the sail starts to fill again on the new tack, you will already be sitting in the correct position. This manœuvre is also called going about.

21

2 *Gybing* This means that you turn away from the wind. To do this, you pull the tiller towards you; the dinghy bears away from the wind, and when the wind is astern you must next take hold of the sheet as close to the boom as possible and pull the boom and sail over on to the other

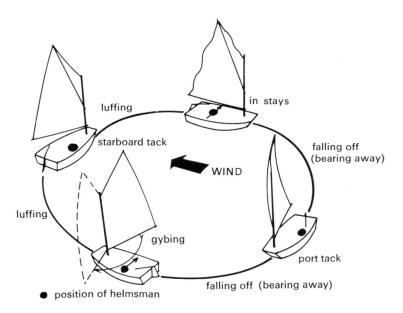

luffing

in stays

starboard tack

falling off
(bearing away)

WIND

luffing

gybing

port tack

falling off (bearing away)

● position of helmsman

side; at the same time quickly changing sides yourself. The fresher the wind, the quicker you have to be, or else the dinghy will heel over sharply and might even capsize. As a beginner, you should not try to gybe in a fresh wind.

How to set your sail

You have to adjust the angle of your sail to suit the direction of the wind — this is very important, and you will soon notice that your dinghy's speed depends on how well you set the sail. Try this experiment: steer a steady course with the sheet at first hard in so that the boom is near the centre-line of the boat; now ease the sheet slowly—that is, let it out bit by bit—and as you do so, keep an eye on the part of the sail next to the mast. When it starts to flap a little (we say that the luff of the sail is lifting), stop easing the sheet and pull it in a bit, and your sail is now correctly set. More about this later.

Sailing close-hauled and tacking

You cannot sail straight towards the wind—the sail would not fill—but you can work your way up wind by tacking. Let us see how this is done.

First sail on the starboard tack, steering as close to the wind as you can without the sail flapping and the dinghy slowing down (that would be pinching which, as you will soon find out, gets you nowhere!) You are now close-hauled on the starboard tack. When you have gone far

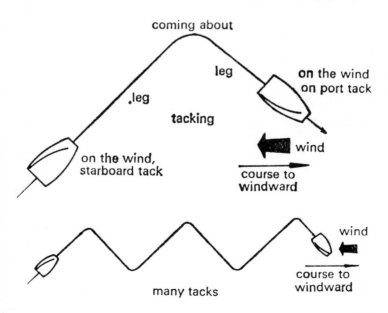

enough — and that is where experience comes in — go about onto the other tack. Sometimes you will have to make many small tacks to beat to windward, at other times it will be better to make long tacks; it all depends on the weather and other conditions. Sailing close-hauled is sometimes called being hard on the wind and the tacks you make are sometimes called boards. Like the Optimist dinghy, many of our sailing terms came to England from Scandinavia and they sound strange at first, but you will soon be as good at talking about sailing as you will be at sailing your Optimist dinghy.

Sailing close-hauled is perhaps the most difficult point of sailing. You will find that it is difficult to choose the ideal course and position for your sail; these are best found by hard training with other Optimist helmsmen. As a general rule, when you are close-hauled the after end of the boom should point towards the corner of the transom (the quarter). Try starting with the sail set like this, then haul in on the sheet and you will discover that it is now possible to sail a little closer to the wind but that you will go more slowly. So with the sheet hard in you shorten the distance you must go as you beat to windward, but you have also reduced your speed. On the other hand, if you ease your sheet and allow the dinghy to fall off from the wind a little, your Optimist will sail faster — but you now have farther to go. Only practice will enable you to find the golden mean. Beginners often make the same mistake

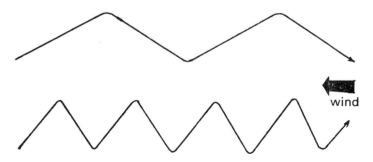

wind

of trying to sail too close to the wind, pointing high but making very slow progress; remember to keep the dinghy moving all the time.

If the wind was constant in direction and strength, sailing close-hauled would not be so difficult (nor would it be as interesting). In fact, the wind is changing in speed and direction all the time, and you must react to these changes, making small adjustments with your tiller. When the wind changes direction and blows more onto the side of your dinghy (or frees) you ease the tiller to come close to the wind again. On the other hand, when the wind direction changes the other way and starts to blow more from the bow, you must quickly pull the tiller towards you to make the dinghy fall off a little from the wind (you have been headed); if the direction has changed a lot, it may be better to go about onto the other tack. The speed or strength of

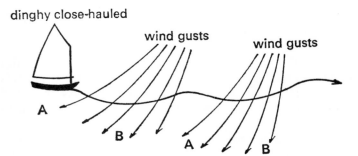

At A dinghy is headed and bears away
At B wind frees and dinghy can luff again

the wind changes too, and you will find that you can sail closer to a stronger wind. The waves also make a difference, for they tend to slow you down. When the waves are small you can sail close to the wind, but when they are larger it pays to bear away a little, ease your sheets and keep up your speed.

So when you are sailing close-hauled you don't just sail

one course; you keep adjusting your course as the conditions change, all the time trying to keep your dinghy sailing fast and as close to the eye of the wind as you can. You will learn to watch closely for changes in the wind and also to keep an eye on the shape and size of the waves.

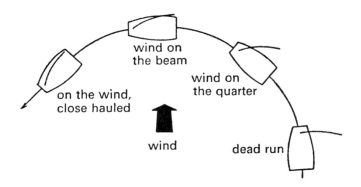

Sailing off the wind

That is to say, when you are not close-hauled. Your aim is now to sail on a constant course and to ease the sheets until your dinghy goes as fast as possible. As the wind changes in direction, you will have to ease out or haul in the sheet a little to get the best result. When the wind is astern, you will have the sheet so far out that the sail is at right angles to the dinghy. This is called running. When the wind is on the beam you are reaching.

The shape of the sail in fresh and light winds

When the wind is fresh, you should try to flatten the sail, while when the wind is light you need to make the sail more baggy. How is this done? You flatten the sail by pulling it out tightly along the boom and mast (but not beyond the black bands); by easing the downhaul and the outhaul on the boom, you make the sail fuller.

The daggerboard

If your Optimist did not have a daggerboard, it would only sail with the wind. The daggerboard is needed to stop the dinghy drifting sideways (making leeway) and enables you to sail on a reach or close-hauled. But you don't need the daggerboard down all the time. When you are running (with the wind astern) it is better to lift the daggerboard — then you go faster. In a fresh wind, even when you are reaching or close-hauled, it still pays to raise the daggerboard a little — you will find that the steering becomes easier and the speed increases. Finally, if you get stuck in irons, that is to say head to wind, you will find that by lifting the daggerboard, partly or completely, the dinghy can be made to fall off from the wind, and you can get under way again.

Weather helm and lee helm

Normally, you have to keep the tiller towards the windward (or weather) side of the dinghy to keep on a steady course; release the tiller and the dinghy turns up into the wind. Ideally, you should need only a little weather helm. If you need a lot, it is hard work for you and, even more important, the rudder acts as a brake and slows you down. The dinghy is then said to be heavy on the rudder and this can be due to

1 Mast raked too far aft. Move the mast step a little aft; this moves the sail forwards and the dinghy will not luff so hard.
2 Badly shaped sail — with the leech not flat enough. Only the sailmaker can put this right.
3 You may not be in the right place. When the wind is fresh, and the dinghy heels hard over, the curved side cutting through the water will make the dinghy luff. You must sit out more on the weather side to reduce the heel.

You should not have to use lee helm to maintain a steady course.

27

Coming alongside

Even though the Optimist is a small dinghy and easy to stop, you must be careful when you return to the jetty or shore after sailing. Of course, you will never steer for the shore at full speed with the sail full of wind! You stop by turning up into the wind and letting your sheets fly. If the wind direction does not allow you to stop where you want to tie up, you should aim to stop a little up wind; the wind will then drift you to where you want to be. Sometimes, when wind and tide are together, it will be more seamanlike to lower your mast and sail when you have luffed up.

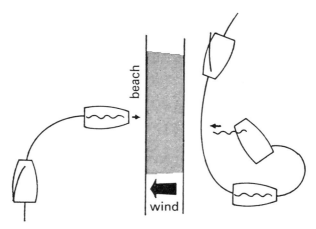

Capsizing

If you should capsize your Optimist, there is one vital rule to remember—never leave the dinghy. Stay with your boat until help comes. Of course, you may not need any help to get back in and sail on. If you do need help, you can pass your gear to the rescue boat while you are getting the water out of your dinghy. If for some reason it is not possible to bail out, then you will have to tow the dinghy ashore by means of its painter; remove the centre-board first.

Most capsizes happen on a run—and often because the sail is too far out in a heavy wind. So practise to find out how far you can let the sheet go while still maintaining full control.

You can also capsize when you are sailing close-hauled, or on a reach, if the wind pressure on the sail is too great and the boat is pushed hard over. In this case, reduce the pressure by easing out the sheets and 'spilling' some of the wind. For this reason, always keep the sheet in hand so that you can react quickly to a sudden gust.

Sailing faster

Once you have overcome the basic problems and you feel that you are in command of the dinghy and not a mere passenger, you will want to improve your sailing technique. You will learn a lot by watching more experienced helmsmen and trying to out-sail them. Here are a few points to bear in mind.

Beating In a fresh wind, the boat will go better if you can keep it from heeling. Sit up on the gunwale and move your weight in or out as the wind strength changes. Toe straps and a tiller extension will help you balance the boat.

In a lighter wind it pays to sit further forward in the boat than usual and in a stronger wind further aft.

On a run You can go faster by heeling the dinghy to windward—see the picture opposite page 16—provided that there is enough wind to hold the boom up like that. In this way, you will also reduce the area of the hull in contact with the water and that cuts down the drag. Be careful though, for you can very easily capsize until you have got the knack of sailing this way!

Maintaining the Optimist dinghy

By the end of the summer sailing season your dinghy will have had a hard time. Sun, salt water and scratches combine to make the hull look grey and sad. A varnished hull is the easiest finish to maintain and this is the way to set about it. First give the hull a good wash with a household liquid soap and fresh water; take out oil or tar stains with petrol. You will need to take out all the fittings and buoyancy so that you can work on all the internal surfaces of the hull.

Next sand the hull down. Wet and dry paper is best and it doesn't make a dusty mess. Wet and dry works best with lots of water and remember to rinse the hull well afterwards so that the powder does not dry into the wood. For an extra fine finish you can use turpentine instead of water and afterwards dry off with a cloth.

Having sanded down thoroughly, check to see if any minor repairs are needed so that you can be sure the boat will be sound for the new season; for example, after tough racing the mast thwart and its bulkhead may no longer be completely secure.

Varnishing

It is important to use good varnish and a good quality brush. You must first touch-up the places where the bare wood shows; do this with varnish which has been thinned with white spirit. Before varnishing the hull, make sure that you have removed all the dust; a cloth damped with turpentine is the best for this. Only put a little varnish on the brush each time and apply it to the dinghy with long smooth strokes.

If you haven't varnished before, try to get someone to show you how it is done. How many coats will be needed? Well, that depends on the state of the dinghy, but two to three coats outside and one to two inside is usual.

Painted dinghies

The method is similar. If the paintwork is not too badly damaged, you can spot paint the bare places (with paint to match) and then gently rub down with wet paper—using water, not turpentine—before putting on the top coat.

Always remember to clean your brush soon after use. They're expensive items and if not cleaned out thoroughly after use, before the paint or varnish has dried, they can soon be ruined. White spirit is a good cleaning agent.

GRP Optimists

A GRP dinghy is generally easier to maintain because it should only need regular polishing, but be careful to avoid scratches as they are not easy to cure. Shallow ones can be removed by using rubbing paste and repolishing. Don't rub too hard or you may damage the gel coat.

Storing your dinghy for the winter

At the end of the sailing season, give your Optimist an extra-careful wash and then take the dinghy and all its gear home. If you have to leave it at the club or in a boat-yard, it is best to store it upside-down resting on some bricks, which keeps it off the ground and lets air circulate. Place a canvas or plastic cover over it, using a frame of old planks to keep the cover off the dinghy.

Rules for avoiding collision at sea

Below are given, and illustrated, the most important of the international Rules of the Road. You must know these before you sail.

When two sailing boats approach one another and there is danger of a collision, one of them has to give way and keep clear of the other. The drawings show you how the rules work.

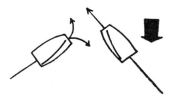

If they are on opposite tacks the boat on the port tack must alter course to keep clear of the boat on the starboard tack.

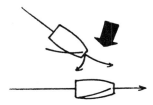

If they are on the same tack, the windward boat must keep clear of the other.

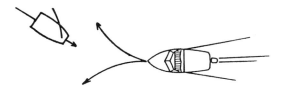

A power boat must always keep clear of a sailing boat. There are exceptions to this rule: when you are cruising you should not get in the way of commercial vessels, and you must give way to large ships in narrow channels and in harbours—and of course to power-boat races!

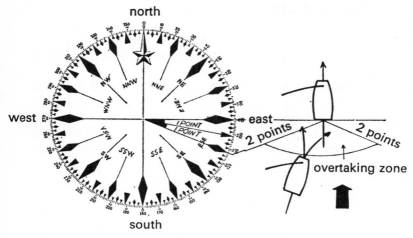

The compass rose is divided in to 360 degrees, or 32 points.

When a boat approaches from a direction more than two points abaft the beam of another, it is said to be overtaking and must keep clear. This applies even in the unlikely event of a sailing boat overtaking a motor boat.

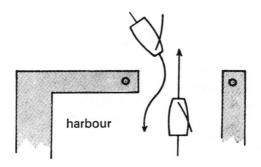

A boat entering a harbour must keep out of the way of one which is leaving.

Speed, tidal stream and wind

A boat's speed is measured in knots: one knot is one sea mile per hour, and a sea mile, or nautical mile, is 6080 feet (2027 yards) or 1853 metres.

The speed of the tidal stream is also measured in knots. When you are sailing, it is important to be able to judge the direction and speed of the tidal stream. Buoys, or other sea marks will help you to do so as you can see in the diagram below, which shows the effect of the tidal stream on an anchored buoy.

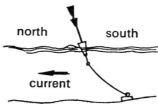

We refer to the direction of the tidal stream by the way the water is going. Above, there is a *north*-going stream which you may sometimes hear described as a northerly set. On the other hand, a south wind is one blowing *from* the south.

The wind speed may be given in various ways. The Beaufort scale is still probably the most usual way of describing the wind, but the other scales are all used at times. Beaufort, by the way, was an English Admiral who established his scale in the year 1806. When the weather forecast says that the wind will be north Force 5, you can expect an exciting sail. On page 35 you will find a table of wind speeds showing the various scales, and on the following pages there are diagrams of different types of sailing vessel and hull form; keep your eyes open while you are sailing and you will see examples of most, if not all, of these.

Rounding the windward mark: as 443 comes round, he is preparing to gybe for the run to the next mark (see page 22).

Photograph by Eileen Ramsay

Jockeying for position at the start.

Photograph by Eileen Ramsay

Table of Wind Forces

Beaufort Number	Limits of Wind Speed in knots	Descriptive Terms	Meaning	Probable Height of Waves in feet
0	Less than 1	Calm	Sea like a mirror: no sailing!	—
1	1—3	Light air	Ripples — Optimists ghost along	$\frac{1}{4}$
2	4—6	Light breeze	Small glassy wavelets. Optimists sailing down wind may be heeled to windward	$\frac{1}{2}$
3	7—10	Gentle breeze	Wave crests begin to break. A good wind for beginners	2
4	11—16	Moderate breeze	Waves getting longer. Sit out when beating to windward	$3\frac{1}{2}$
5	17—21	Fresh breeze	Lots of white horses: a hard sailing wind	6
6	22—27	Strong breeze	Only the most experienced will sail in this wind. You need to adjust your course to the large waves and avoid over-straining your spars	$9\frac{1}{2}$

The rest of the scale is NOT Optimist weather, but the dinghies may take off from the dinghy park if they are not well secured.

7	28—33	Near gale	Foam forms in lines downwind	$13\frac{1}{2}$
8	34—40	Gale	Spindrift (frothy foam) breaks from crests	18
9	41—47	Strong gale	Crests of waves begin to topple	23
10	48—55	Storm	Crests topple heavily	29
11	56—63	Violent storm	Sea completely covered with froth	37
12 and over	64+	Hurricane	Air filled with driving spray	

Do you know?

Sailing rigs

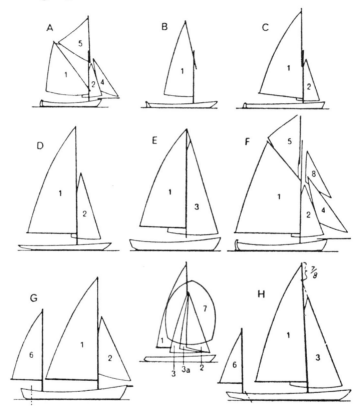

A Sprit	1 Mainsail
B Lug	2 Jib
C Gunter	3 Genoa
D Bermudan	3a No 2 Genoa
E Masthead	4 Outer jib
F Gaff	5 Topsail
G Ketch (rudder aft of the mizzen mast)	6 Mizzen
	7 Spinnaker
H Yawl (rudder forward of the mizzen mast)	8 Flying jib

These and 8 are all foresails

Hulls

hull types

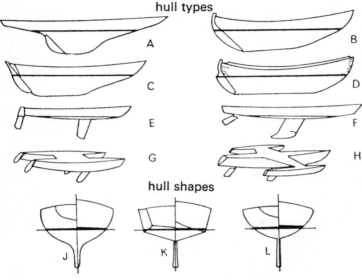

hull shapes

A Counter stern
B Canoe stern
C Transom stern
D Double-ender
E Centreboard dinghy
F Fin-keeled boat with spade rudder

G Catamaran
H Trimaran
J Keel boat
K Hard chine
L Round bilge

construction methods

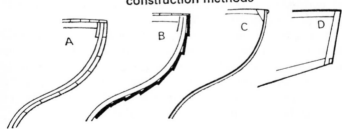

A Carvel built
B Clinker built
C Glassfibre clad (three layer glassfibre foam sandwich)
D Hard chine. Usually built with marine ply, sometimes sheathed with glassfibre, or glassfibre alone.

37

Racing

When you have overcome your first problems and can handle your Optimist dinghy, then there's every chance that you will want to start racing with your friends. Racing is good fun and is also the best way to become an expert helmsman.

Preparation

Before entering a race, you must be sure that your dinghy and all its gear is in good order. The bottom of the hull must be clean and smooth. You will find it pays to sand and re-varnish several times in the season, in fact, those who are very keen on racing water-sandpaper their hulls before each race! Check the gear carefully and rectify any faults—it is very annoying to have to retire from a race because of failure in a defective item of gear.

If it is possible, set the sail before you launch the dinghy. Walk around the dinghy and check that all is well. The sail must be firmly secured to the mast and the boom and the sprit strop must be correctly adjusted. You should adjust the sail to suit the strength of the wind—put more fullness into the sail in light winds and flatten it for fresh winds. Check to see that the sheet runs easily.

Remember to read the racing programme and sailing instructions thoroughly and listen carefully to the briefing; if you don't understand, ask!

Be sure to get out to the start in good time so that you can get used to the conditions and can judge the wind, sea and stream. Notice where the marks are and pay particular attention to the direction of the first mark from the starting-line. All this will help you form a plan in your mind for the start and for the rest of the race.

Sailing instruction and courses

Printed instructions are issued in advance for important races, and these give you all the information you need.

The course can be marked out in several different ways; examples of some of the most usual types of course are shown in the diagrams below.

The turning-points on the course are called marks and these are usually in the form of buoys which often carry flags. The starting and finishing lines may be between two buoys. Whenever possible, the first leg of the course and the final leg will both be to windward, so that you have to tack across the lines.

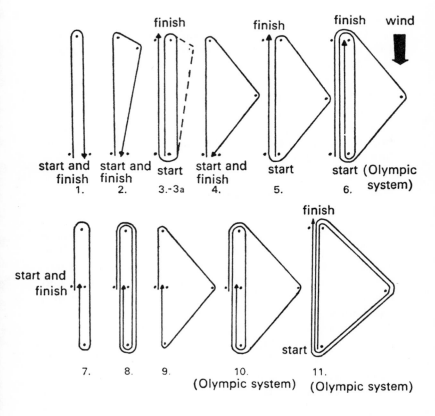

On the bridge ashore or on the committee boat, the following signs will usually be displayed:

to show that the race will take place at the advertised time—the club pennant.

if the start is to be delayed—a red and white striped pennant (the answering pennant).

Quite often a numbered board will be used to indicate the course being sailed, and a large arrow may be displayed to show the direction of the start.

Starting signals

At ten minutes to the start, the warning signal is hoisted; it takes the form of a class flag (usually flag o). At the same time a gun is fired—or some other sound signal is made, to draw attention to the flag.

At five minutes to the start, the preparatory signal is hoisted (flag p) and another gun is fired.

Exactly five minutes after the preparatory signal, both flags are lowered and the race starts. A gun is again fired but should it fail to go off, you must remember that the flag signal counts.

Racing rules for Optimist helmsmen

Just as there are traffic rules on land, there are rules on the water. If you are not racing, you must follow the rules for avoiding collisions which were given on page 31. When you are racing there are rather more complicated rules, which are needed for all the situations which arise when many dinghies are sailing together in confined waters and which make for good sport.

The racing rules are international, so you use the same rules wherever you race in the world. In this section the official wording has been used as much as possible, as this will help you when you have to protest.

As there are rather a lot of rules, the most important ones have been selected. Learn these carefully and you will find that they will be sufficient for you in most of your races in an Optimist dinghy.

Explanation of terms

Before you can understand the rules, you must know the meaning of the terms which are used. The diagrams will help.

Luffing   Altering course towards the wind until head to wind.

Tacking   A yacht is *tacking* from the moment she is beyond head to wind until she has *borne away*, if beating to windward, to a *close-hauled* course; if not beating to windward, to the course on which her mainsail has filled.

Bearing away   Altering course away from the wind until a yacht begins to gybe. Also called falling off the wind.

Gybing   A yacht begins to *gybe* at the moment when, with the wind aft, the foot of her mainsail crosses her centreline and completes the *gybe* when the mainsail has filled on the other tack.

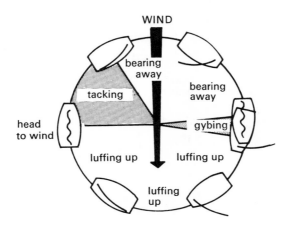

Clear astern
Clear ahead
Overlap

A yacht is *clear astern* of another when her hull and equipment in normal position are abaft an imaginery line projected abeam from the aftermost point of the other's hull and equipment in normal position. The

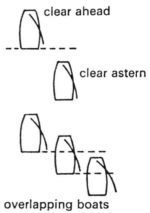

clear ahead

clear astern

overlapping boats

other yacht is *clear ahead.* The yachts *overlap* if neither is *clear astern*; or if, although one is *clear astern*, an intervening yacht *overlaps* them both. These terms apply to yachts on the same tack and also to those on opposite tacks which are rounding or passing marks or obstructions.

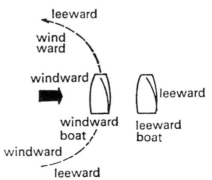

leeward

wind
ward

windward

windward
boat

windward

leeward

leeward

leeward
boat

Leeward and Windward The *leeward* side of a yacht is that on which she is, or, if *luffing* head to wind, was carrying her mainsail. The opposite side is the *windward* side.

When neither of two yachts on the same *tack* is *clear astern*, the one on the *leeward* side of the other is the *leeward* yacht. The other is the *windward* yacht.

On a tack A yacht is *on a tack*, except when she is *tacking* or *gybing*. A yacht is on the tack (*starboard* or *port*) corresponding to her *windward* side.

Proper course A *proper course* is any course which a yacht might sail after the starting signal, in the absence of the other yachts affected, to *finish* as quickly as possible.

The proper course need not be directly towards the next mark. For example, with a tidal stream as shown, the dinghy on its proper course is sailing closer to the wind than the course to the next mark.

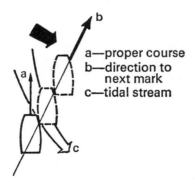

a—proper course
b—direction to next mark
c—tidal stream

Marks A *mark* is any object specified in the sailing instructions which a yacht must pass on a required side.

Note that marks must be passed in the right order and on the correct side. If you make a mistake and round the mark on the wrong side, you are allowed to correct your error like this:

In this race, marks must be left to port. A rounds correctly, B fails to correct his mistake, C corrects his mistake properly.

What happens if you touch a mark? You must either protest against the dinghy which, contrary to the rules, has caused you to do so, or you may make a complete circuit round the mark. You have no 'rights' during this manoeuvre, so be careful to keep out of the way of all other dinghies while you round the mark again.

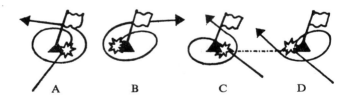

A Correct re-rounding after touching a port mark.
B Correct re-rounding after touching a starboard mark.
C Correct re-rounding after touching the port mark on the start or finishing line.
D Correct re-rounding after touching the starboard mark on the start or finishing line.
It does not matter if you merely touch the mark's mooring.

Starting A yacht *starts* when, after her starting signal, any part of her hull, crew or equipment first crosses the starting line in the direction of the first *mark*.

A dinghy which has started too soon must return and start again. While returning, it must give way to all other competitors. Normally, all you have to do is to sail back until you are clear behind the line and then restart, but you may be required to sail back around the end of the line.

Finishing A yacht *finishes* when any part of her hull, or of her crew or equipment in normal position, crosses the finishing line from the direction of the last *mark*.

A signal will be made as each dinghy finishes. Be careful not to touch a mark on the finishing line nor to break any of the other rules until you are clear of the line and of other competitors.

The sailing rules

From the time the preparatory signal is given (normally five minutes before the start, but sometimes less in Optimist races) until you are clear of the finishing line, you must be careful not to break any of the following rules; don't confuse the rule numbers here with those of the IYRU rules.

Don't forget also that you are expected to win by fair sailing, using the wind and your skill; tiller waggling is not considered to be fair.

Opposite tack rule

1 A *port*-tack yacht shall keep clear of a *starboard*-tack yacht. You must keep your eyes open when you are

on the port tack. Be careful to pass well ahead of a starboard-tack dinghy; if in doubt, it is safer to give way and pass astern—or go about in good time.

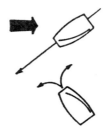

When two dinghies on opposite tacks meet, the one on port tack must keep out of the way.

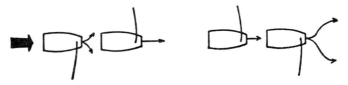

The rule also applies when a dinghy catches up with another from astern.

Same tack rules

2 A *windward yacht* shall keep clear of *leeward* yacht.

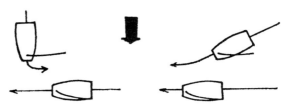

When dinghies on the same tack meet, the windward one must keep clear.

3 A dinghy *clear astern* shall keep clear of a dinghy *clear ahead*.

4 *Luffing*. The rules are given step by step below.

4A A dinghy *clear ahead* or a *leeward* dinghy may *luff* as she pleases, as far as head to wind, to try to prevent a windward dinghy overtaking.

The leeward dinghy may not luff, however, if the helmsman in the windward dinghy is forward of the mast of the leeward dinghy.

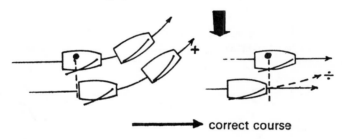

correct course

When the windward dinghy's helmsman is aft of the leeward dinghy's mast, luffing is allowed.

When the windward dinghy's helmsman is ahead of the leeward dinghy's mast, luffing is not allowed.

4B The leeward dinghy must turn back on to her proper course as she loses luffing rights.

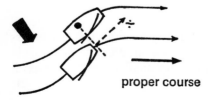

proper course

The leeward dinghy has now lost its right to luff and must immediately return on to the proper course.

47

The helmsman of the windward dinghy should call 'mast abeam' when that is the case.

4C Once a leeward dinghy loses luffing rights, it may not luff again until it either has drawn clear ahead or has fallen off to leeward so that more than two boats' lengths separate them.

4D An overtaking dinghy which establishes an overlap to leeward of another may not luff. Luffing rights can only be obtained, as mentioned in point C, by sailing clear ahead or more than two boat lengths to leeward.

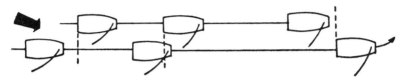

By rule 4D the dinghy overtaking to leeward in this diagram does not have overtaking rights until she draws clear ahead of the other.

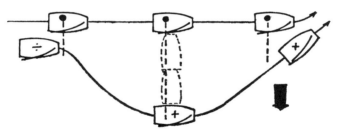

Similarly if the dinghy which is overtaking to leeward sails out to more than two boats' lengths to leeward of the other, she obtains luffing rights as soon as the windward helmsman finds himself astern of the leeward dinghy's mast.

E *Luffing two or more boats* A dinghy shall not luff unless she has the right to luff all the dinghies which would be affected. In which case, they shall all respond even if an intervening dinghy would not otherwise have the right to luff.

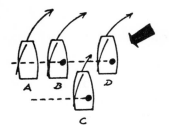

A has the right to luff as all the helmsmen are abaft its mast. Although *C* would not have luffing rights on its own over *D*, all must luff together when *A* luffs. (See rule 4E.)

F Before a dinghy has started and cleared the starting line, any luff on her part must be carried out slowly.
After the starting signal, the leeward boat may luff slowly on to her proper course no matter what her position.

5 *Sailing below a proper course* A dinghy which is on a free leg of the course after having started and cleared the starting line shall not sail below her *proper course* when she is clearly within three lengths of either a *leeward dinghy* or a dinghy *clear astern* which is steering a course to pass to leeward. This means that a windward boat cannot bear away from the wind to prevent another passing it on the lee side.

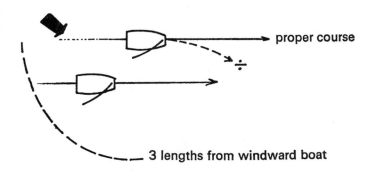

proper course

3 lengths from windward boat

Changing tack rules

6 A dinghy which is either *tacking* or *gybing* shall keep
   clear of a dinghy *on a tack*.
   Look back to the definitions of tacking and gybing.
7 A dinghy shall neither *tack* nor *gybe* so close to another
   that the other has not room to keep clear by altering
   course after the tack or gybe is completed.

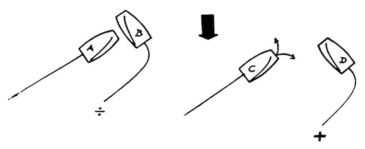

A has not sufficient room to keep clear. *C* can keep clear.

Rounding a mark

8 When dinghies are about to round a mark, an outside
   dinghy must give each dinghy overlapping her on the inside room to round the mark.

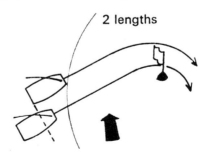

The inside dinghy has established an overlap before the
leading dinghy is within two lengths of the mark; it has therefore the right to room round the mark. (See rule 11 also.)

9 When the dinghies are on a leg of the course with the wind free, an inside dinghy with an overlap must be given room no matter which tack it is on.

This rule is an exception to the Opposite Tack Rule 1.

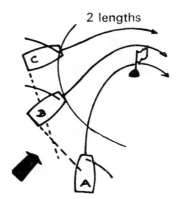

2 lengths

9 Even though *A* is on the port tack, she must be given room, having established an overlap before *C* is within two lengths of the mark. *B* must keep well clear as *A* will gybe as she rounds the mark.

10 When two boats on opposite tacks beat up to a mark, or one boat will have to tack to round the mark, the port-tack boat must give way (point 1).

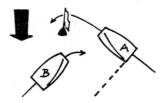

10 Although *B* overlaps *A*, she cannot claim room to round the mark. In this case Rule 1 applies.

11 The overlap must be obtained before the leading dinghy is within two lengths of the mark.

Note These rules about rounding marks also apply to obstructions like jetties or other objects which cannot be passed on either side.

12 Exception to the rounding rules.
   When approaching the starting line, a leeward dinghy
   is not obliged to give room to allow a windward dinghy
   to pass to leeward of the starting-mark; but after the
   starting signal, she must not sail higher than close-hauled
   or than the course to the first mark.

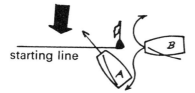

Even though *B* overlaps
A, she cannot demand
room from *A* to pass the
starting mark.

Team racing rules

When you are racing in a team, you must observe the normal racing rules. However there are a few extra rules of
which the most important are the following:

   (i) A dinghy shall neither sail above nor below her
proper course to manœuvre against a dinghy sailing
another leg of the course.

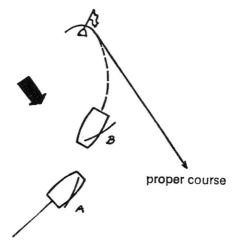

proper course

B must not sail higher than her proper course to hinder
opponent *A*.

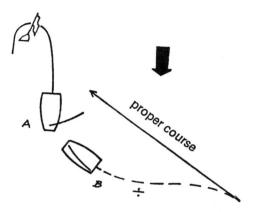

B must not sail below her proper course to hinder opponent *A*.

(ii) Except to protect her own or a team mate's position, a dinghy in one team which is completing the last leg of the course shall not manœuvre against a dinghy in another team which has no opponent astern of her.

(iii) Right of way may be waived by team mates, provided that in doing so no opponent is baulked.

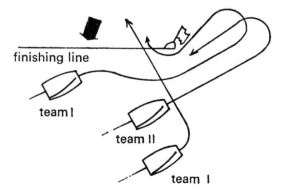

This drawing shows you how you can use the rule above to gain first and second places for your team instead of first and third.

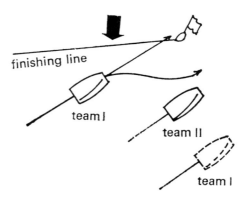

finishing line

team I

team II

team I

Note that the Team I helmsman near the line must not interfere with his Team II opponent unless there is another member of Team I following (the dotted dinghy in the diagram).

Scoring The recommended scoring system is: $\frac{3}{4}$ point for the winner, 2 points for second, 3 points for third, etc. A boat which cannot finish because of a gear failure gains the same points as the number of boats sailing. Failure to finish for any other reason, as well as retiring after a rule infringement, means another point, while disqualification results in a score of 4 points more than the number of competitors.

Infringements of the rules

You should always try to keep to the racing rules. If you do break one of the rules you should retire from the race or accept an alternative penalty. Disqualification may be the result of a protest by one of the other helmsmen, or may be imposed by the race committee who themselves saw that a rule had not been kept.

When to protest No one should try to win a race simply by protesting against an infringement of the rules which has not affected the finishing order. On the other hand a protest should not be regarded as an unfriendly act; there are often real doubts as to who is in the right and the question can then best be resolved by means of a protest. This is the way to learn more about the rules and the way they apply during races.

How to protest A helmsman who wants to protest against another dinghy must tell the race officer as soon as possible after crossing the finishing line. Then, at the end of the race, he must fill in a protest form giving the position of the boats at the time of the incident, the reason for the protest and the names and sail numbers of any witnesses. The protest committee will then be able to see the witnesses before they leave for home. The committee then hears each person in turn and by asking questions tries to find out just what happened and so decides if the protest is justified.

Informing the other helmsman It is very important to tell the other helmsman that you think he has broken a rule and that you are going to protest. You must do this at the time; just call out 'protest'. He will know what you mean! He may decide that you are right and that he should retire; it also makes sure that he knows that he will be needed to give evidence after the race and can take careful note of the facts and possible witnesses—otherwise he might leave the area of the club when he gets ashore, and the prize-giving would be delayed. To make sure that helmsmen do not protest without first thinking about the rules, you may have to pay a deposit when you fill in the protest form. If the committee finds that you were correct, your deposit will be returned, but if you are wrong, you lose the deposit.

Some hints on racing tactics

What is meant by tactics? Suppose that a number of similar boats start together and sail exactly the same course.

The helmsman who comes first to the finishing line will be the one who has made the best use of all the opportunities that he met during the race; he has used the best tactics.

Points to consider

When beating to windward, have you:
tacked at the right place,
used your 'dirty wind' and wind shadow to slow other boats,
made the best use of the tidal stream,
sailed where there was most wind,
chosen the best position coming up to the marks,
and kept a close eye on the changes of wind?

Dealing with all these tactical problems makes racing fun, and demands quick thinking. It would be impossible to teach you all there is to know about tactics, you will learn best as a result of your own experience. Nevertheless, it should help if you understand the three most important defensive measures described below.

1 *The safe lee bow position* If you place your dinghy close to the lee bow of your opponent, the wind will flow off your sail and 'backwind' his sail—if you do it properly, that is,

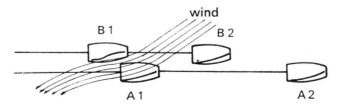

A 1 in the safe lee position, B 1 backwinded; so A forges ahead and B is left astern and they are soon in the positions A 2 and B 2.

and it is harder than it may sound. Your opponent then drops astern since the wind is no longer driving him along. What should the windward boat do when caught like this? He should tack at once before he loses his speed.

2 *Placing your boat ahead of a close-hauled opponent* As you can see in the diagram below, the wind is deflected by your sail and strikes your opponent closer to the bow; he is headed. If he remains on this tack, he will have to bear away and will probably lose speed as well. How should he react? Once again, the best thing would be to go about onto the other tack.

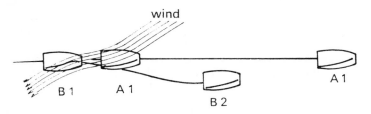

B 1 is headed by the wind because of A 1. B bears away and drops astern of A, so that they reach the positions A 1 and B 2.

3 *Covering with your wind shadow* In the next diagram you can see how a close-hauled dinghy can place itself to use the wind shadow to slow down an opponent. Similarly the second diagram opposite shows a dinghy taking the wind from another ahead on the run. In each case the wind shadow extends about three boats' lengths.

To get out of the difficulty, the close-hauled dinghy can either tack or bear away a little to clear the dirty wind. The dinghy which is being overtaken on the run has also two alternatives: either to luff a little and move out to port clear of the wind shadow, or stay on course and gybe. (In this case, the latter would be a dangerous thing to do; can you see why?)

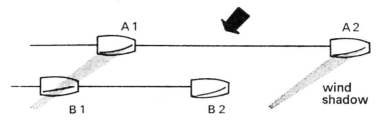

B 1 is blanketed by A 1 and so loses way while A forges
ahead until they are in positions B 2 and A 2.

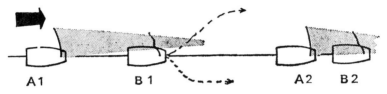

B 1 has again lost his wind because of A 1. B can overcome
the problem in one of two ways as shown; if he does nothing
A catches up and they are soon in positions A 2, B 2.
(A must now be careful!)

Starting

1 *Windward start* It is well said that a good start is a race
half won. To start well you must watch the time carefully
and judge your position so that your dinghy crosses the line
a second after the signal, going at full speed with a free
wind, and further that you cross the line at the best place.
When you are taking part in a race with many other
dinghies, that will be an art indeed! Well before the starting
signal, see how the first mark lies from the line; one end of
the line may be clearly nearer to the mark, but if that is the
port end be careful about deciding on starting on the port
tack – you would have to give way to all starboard-tack
boats. In fact, when there are many dinghies in the race, it
doesn't matter so much where you start as that you get a
free wind. You want to avoid losing your wind to another

boat or being headed by a boat on your lee bow which, as explained before, would backwind your sail. Often the competitors bunch together at what seems to be the better end of the line; few will get a good start. So shortly before the start try to work out where the crush will be and aim to start elsewhere on the line and so get a free wind. The main rules for starting to windward are – starboard tack and clear wind. When possible, the start is to windward.

Reaching start

Rule: start by the lee mark—provided you can do so accurately and at full speed. This gives you luffing rights over all the others and should put you in the safe lee position. If you are not sure of your timing at the start, it will be better to start at the windward mark.

Broad reach start

Rule: start by the windward mark. If you start to leeward you will not be able to break through the lee of the other boats because of the wind shadow.

Running start

Rule: start on the port tack if the first mark is to be left to port, on the starboard tack if it is to be left to starboard.

Beating to windward

The signal has been given and the race has started. Particularly at the start of the race it is essential to waste no time. Concentrate on making your boat go as fast as possible—don't look around too much at the other boats. Later on when you have spread out a bit, will be the time to check on the position and decide on your tactics.

The main rules are: sail with a clean wind the whole time—if you are covered, then tack at once. Don't tack too often—you lose speed each time. Watch for wind changes and tack when you are headed.

If you are in the lead, keep to windward of the others, and cover by tacking as they do.

On the other hand, when you find yourself lagging behind, it will probably pay you to do the opposite to the leaders. For example you can try the other side of the bay where the wind may be better. Otherwise all you can do is grit your teeth and hang on, keep a free wind and watch for the other helmsmen's mistakes; they may, for instance, overstand the mark and so lengthen their course to the mark. Try to sail on the tack which points you closest to your mark.

Broad reach and running

Taking the opponents' wind plays a large part on this point of sailing, but beginners often make the mistake of thinking that all you have to do is cover the dinghy directly in front. The leader tends to draw to one side to clear his wind and the others follow—this merely means that all sail farther to the next mark.

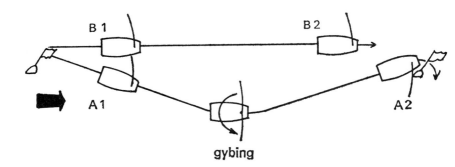

gybing

On the other hand, it pays to remember that your dinghy sails faster with the wind on the quarter; two broad reaches, gybing half-way to the mark, may get you to the mark more quickly than a dead run, particularly in light winds.

Rounding marks

Many races have been won by clever tactics at the marks.

When you beat up to the windward mark, it is important to arrive on the starboard tack. Rule 10 on page 51 shows you why. This applies particularly when you can foresee that a number of dinghies are likely to arrive at the mark together. If you were on port tack, you would probably have to go about or gybe. This would waste time and you would also find it very difficult to keep out of the way of all the others (see Rule 6).

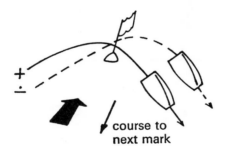

course to
next mark

Do not round a mark too sharply – that would reduce your speed. Rather you should aim to round smoothly, adjusting the sheet at the same time so that as you leave the mark you are sailing as fast as possible on the next leg of the course. The diagram above shows a lee mark. If you steer too close as you come up to it, you will find yourself well downwind before you get onto the new course. It is better to give yourself a little more room at first and to pass close to the leeward side of the mark as you go round. In this way, you may be able to pass dinghies which were ahead but which round badly; those behind you will be forced to tack as you take their wind.

If several dinghies run down to this mark together, there will be a battle to obtain an overlap and the inside position. Those outside will have to sail wide of the mark and are likely to lose several places. If you cannot win the inside position, it is better to drop back and round properly.

The finishing line

When you are closing the finishing line you must remember in good time which end of the line is nearest, because it would be annoying to let competitors get there first because you have been sailing farther than is necessary.

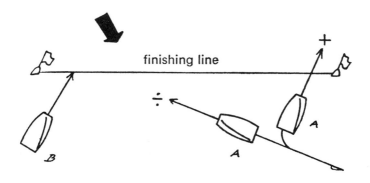

Bigger dinghies

The time will come when your Optimist is too small for you. What then? There is no one answer to this question, for that depends on your ability and preference as well as your weight and, of course, how much you (or your parents) want to spend on your next boat!

The Optimist Class Association in Denmark has been particularly keen to reach agreement on a suitable dinghy for young helmsmen who have learnt their sailing in Optimists and are ready to move on. The growth of the class has made it possible for very many youngsters to take part in national and international sailing and it is suggested that the next age-group would benefit similarly if one or two dinghy types were adopted internationally.

Of course, some will want to sail a dinghy with the very best racing qualities while others will prefer a more stable and less exacting craft. In many cases the decision will turn on the classes which are sailed at the local club. The list of possible dinghies would be almost endless, and more are designed each year, but here are a few suggestions!

Mirror ▶

Length	3 m 30 cm
Beam	1 m 41 cm
Sail area	6·41 sq m
Weight	61·23 kg

A popular, all-purpose dinghy, suitable for all ages. Construction is plywood with glassfibre on the seams, and the dinghy is available in kit form. It has a spinnaker of $65\frac{1}{2}$ sq ft.

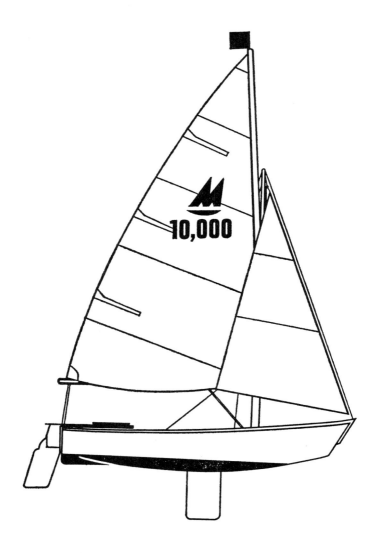

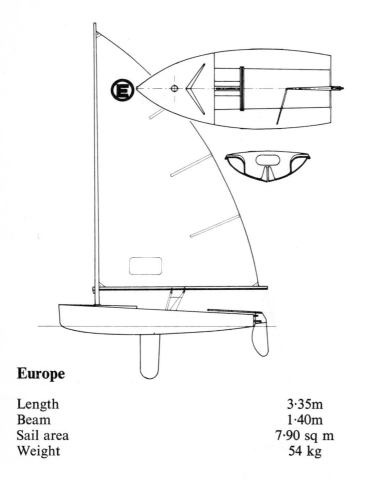

Europe

Length	3·35m
Beam	1·40m
Sail area	7·90 sq m
Weight	54 kg

Originally known as the Europa Moth, Europes conform to the rules of the International Moth class, but they are rather more stable than recent Moth designs. A simple rig, involving few controls, moderate sail area and a light, responsive hull make a boat that is ideal for the good Optimist sailor to move up to. Well established in Europe, these boats are now to be seen in growing numbers in Britain.

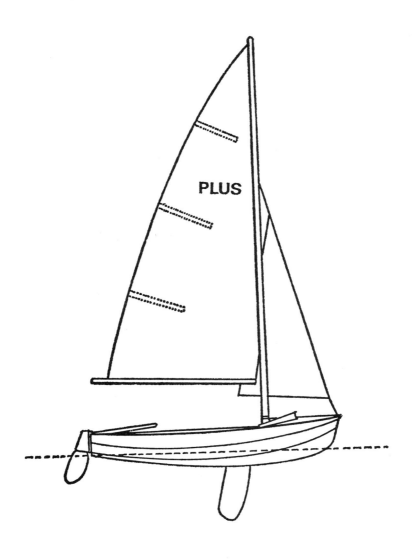

PLUS

◀ **Plus**

Length	3 m 35 cm
Beam	1 m 40 cm
Sail area	6·50 sq m
Weight	65·77 kg

A lively singlehanded or two-man racing dinghy. Safe and dry, the Plus planes fairly easily and is an ideal next-boat for Optimist sailors. The boat was re-designed and modernised in 1968 and is available in plywood or glassfibre.

Flipper ▶

Overall length	4·10 m
Beam	1·32 m
Sail area	10·30 sq m
Hull weight	70 kg

The Flipper is a GRP dinghy designed in Denmark specially for home construction and as a follow-on boat for Optimist sailors.

OK

Length	4 m
Beam	1 m 42 cm
Sail area	8·36 sq m
Weight	72 kg

A singlehanded hard chine dinghy available in plywood or glassfibre. A fast, lively and reasonably priced dinghy, it is very popular in this and other countries. In strong winds it could prove too much to handle for the sailor fresh out of an Optimist. Ideally suited to sailors in late teens.

Graduate

Length	3 m 81 cm
Beam	1 m 44 cm
Sail area	8·36 sq m
Weight	83·91 kg

The hard chine Graduate is of frameless construction and is well suited to home building. The class owners' association organises British schools' and junior championship meetings.

Turtle

Length	3 m 50 cm
Beam	1 m 45 cm
Sail area	8·06 sq m
Weight	53·4 kg

Restricted one-design class. Designed to be equally at home as a car-top family trainer or as an increasingly popular class racing dinghy.

National Solo

Length	3 m 76 cm
Beam	1 m 50 cm
Sail area	8·36 sq m
Weight	68 kg

A popular fast singlehanded dinghy, double chined and light enough to be handled by one man. It has built-in buoyancy and the single sail is fully battened for good control. There is cockpit space for two or three passengers when not racing.

420

Overall length	4·20 m
Beam	1·63 m
Sail area	10·25 sq m
Spinnaker	8·80 sq m

The 420 is another popular two-man boat for young
people.